Sacred Santa Fe

Geomancy, Geometry, and Energetics
of its Churches

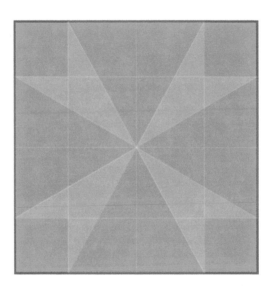

Karen Crowley–Susani
and
Dominique Susani

Triple Enclosure Publishing
Lafayette, Colorado

triple enclosure publishing
www.tripleenclosurepublishing.com

ISBN 978-0-9994807-3-1
Library of Congress Control Number: 2022903094

First published by Triple Enclosure Publishing April 2022
Lafayette, Colorado

For more information about solar and sacred geometry, master builders, tours, classes, and certification training,
visit our website at https://energeticgeometry.com

Design by Karen Crowley-Susani
Illustrations by Dominique Susani and Karen Crowley-Susani
Earth Energy illustrations by Nicolas Susani
Photographs by Ayla Angelo and Karen Crowley-Susani

We dedicate this book to the Master Builders who discovered the special geometrical patterns of Santa Fe and incorporated them into their spiritual masterpieces.

With special gratitude to Nicolas Susani for his intuitive skills and insightful drawings, to Ayla Angelo for helping us complete our research and for taking such lovely photos, and to the incredible Chrissie Heydon for her amazing attention to detail.

Karen and Dominique

Table of Contents

Introduction 1

Chapter One. 3

   the art of building sacred structures. 3

   solar geometry 5

   solsticial rectangle 7

   golden proportion 13

   master builder tradition in action. 15

   the importance of the location 16

   building a sacred place. 20

Chapter Two 27

   history of the mission of san miguel 27

   analysis of subterranean influences 32

   analysis of the geometry of the place 36

   the nave 41

   conclusion. 46

Chapter Three. 47

   history of the shrine of our lady of guadalupe 47

   analysis of subterranean influences 51

   analysis of the geometry of the place 53

conclusion. 57

Chapter Four 58

history of the cathedral of st. francis of assisi 58

analysis of subterranean influences 62

analysis of the geometry of the place 64

orientation 65

geometry of the nave 66

geometry of the transept. 72

geometry of the apse 74

conclusion. 78

Chapter Five. 79

history of the loretto chapel. 79

analysis of the subterranean energies 83

analysis of the geometry of the place 85

the nave 86

the sacristy. 88

geometry of the exterior elevation 89

the staircase. 92

conclusion. 93

Conclusion 94

Appendix. 96

    solsticial rectangles. 96

    santa fe's solsticial rectangle 97

    building churches 98

    dynamic rectangles. 100

    static rectangles. 109

Bibliography 112

35.7° Latitude

Introduction

Santa Fe, New Mexico, has been considered sacred for centuries, even thousands of years. The Anasazi and Pueblo Native Americans called it home and revered the beautiful Sangre de Cristo and Jemez mountain ranges surrounding the city. When the Spaniards arrived in the early 17th century, they named Santa Fe the City of Holy Faith.

What did the Spanish see in this location? Could they feel the sacred energies of the place? Was it the majestic mountain vistas or the beauty of the stars? Or perhaps it was something else, something elusive that also attracted other Christian religions in the mid-1800s, and Eastern religions in the 1900s. New Age people, healers, shamans, artists, bodyworkers, writers, and poets have all flocked to Santa Fe through the years.

Because spirituality is important in the City of Holy Faith, we decided to explore it through the lens of the European Master Builders, and the churches left behind. The Spanish built many churches in New Mexico, and most are in ruins. Still, somehow in Santa Fe, we have a few beautiful examples of surviving sacred structures dedicated to Christian spirituality. These special churches are the Mission of San Miguel, the Shrine of Our Lady of Guadalupe, the Cathedral of St. Francis of Assisi, and the Chapel of Loretto. As you will discover, many spiritual and healing energies are waiting to be explored inside of them.

Cathedral of St. Francis of Assisi, Santa Fe, New Mexico
Photo credit: Ayla Angelo

Chapter One

the art of building sacred structures

The art of building sacred structures is a fascinating subject that spans thousands of years. There is a continuity of study, design, and vision of what can be called sacred through the ages. These special places date back to the Neolithic times and the first solar structures. Through time, the builders of these revered sites came to be called Master Builders in the European Tradition. The Cromlech of Crucuno is one of the oldest solar structures still standing in France.

The Cromlech of Crucuno, Brittany, France
Photo credit: Karen Crowley-Susani

Master Builders were building with an organic geometrical concept, a fusion of solar geometry and the geometry of the golden mean found in nature. The development of life on Earth is related to the sun, which makes all life possible. The sun's rhythm, vibration, warmth, and the quality of its rays make sure that life is abundant on earth. On the other hand, there is a unique geometry found in the growth of living structures. We see it in plants, shells, bones of animals, our cells, and even our DNA. This geometry is associated with the golden ratio, also called the golden mean, divine proportion, golden proportion or golden section. It works as a fractal in all these structures.

The Master Builders since the Neolithic times were aware of this and always tried to mix these two fundamental principles in their constructions; the rhythm of the sun and the golden ratio.

The lineage of building sacred structures in the western world flows through ancient cultures, such as the Sumerians, Dravidians, Hindus, Egyptians, Chinese, Greeks, Romans, and through the Middle Ages and Renaissance. The knowledge and tradition of using solar geometry began to fall into disuse around the beginning of the 19th century.

To understand how churches, cathedrals, and basilicas were conceived and designed, let's take a look inside the world of the European Master Builders and their creations of sacred structures. First of all, we need to look at the concept of solar geometry and understand why it was so important.

solar geometry

The earth's energy is partly produced by itself, through the rotation of its internal core and dynamo effect, and by its relationship with the Sun. It has been established that the Sun nourishes the earth with its radiance, and without it, no life on our planet is possible.

Ancient societies have all recognized this phenomenon. Everywhere in the ancient world, we find evidence of the Sun being omnipresent. It was recognized as one of the most important gods. Some examples of solar deities include the Hindu god Surya, the Egyptian god Ra, Helios was the Greek god of the Sun, and the Incas worshipped Inti. These are just a few of the many examples of the importance placed upon the deification of the Sun.

Ancient cultures also studied the solar rhythm with great interest and precision. This knowledge allowed them to establish agrarian calendars. Highlighted by the most important solar times of the year, these calendars recognized and used the solstices and equinoxes for important celebrations.

These solar calendars were also the beginning of a particular geometry linking the Sun and the Earth together. We can call this phenomena, solar geometry, because it reproduces the rhythm of the sun on the earth. When this rectangular shaped rhythm of the solstices is settled on the earth with

Ra, ancient Sun god of the Egyptians

some weight, it modifies the exchanges between the earth and the cosmos in that place.

Solar geometry modifies the exchanges of energy on the earth's surface in a way that is misunderstood at first. It is for this reason it could be perceived as magic by some. Standard scientific instruments of our times have trouble verifying these modifications as well. Later we will see exactly how the solar rectangle changes the very energy of the place it touches.

Religious establishments kept these techniques of solar geometry secret because if a church was seen as a solar temple, it could be thought of as a contradiction of their beliefs. But for the theologians, this thought was always present as a thread running through their discussions. In some philosophical and theological thoughts, churches were regarded as solar temples. It is true because solar geometry is a geometry that manifests sacred energy. It was widely taught in religious seminaries and monasteries.

solsticial rectangle

Solsticial Rectangles are fascinating structures. They are rectangular shapes found by tracing the sun's position during the solstices. The four corners are connected to the sun; the summer solstice sunrise, summer solstice sunset, winter solstice sunrise, and winter solstice sunset.

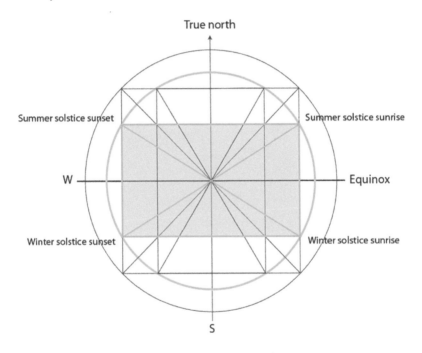

The Solsticial Rectangle

Each latitude has its unique Solsticial Rectangle and ratio between its long and short sides. For example, at the equator, the Solsticial Rectangle has a ratio of 1 ÷ 2.307. At the Tropics of Capricorn and Cancer, the proportion is 1 ÷ 2.097. At the latitude of N31.76, which is Jerusalem, the ratio is 1 ÷ 1.88. At Ephesus at the latitude of N37.95, the proportion is 1.71. Lastly, in Rome, at the latitude of N41.90, the ratio is 1 ÷ 1.58.

Solsticial Rectangle of Jerusalem

In this illustration, you can see that these Solsticial Rectangles are of different shapes and sizes. The different shapes are formed because the angle of the sun changes with latitude. We intentionally used the examples of Jerusalem, Ephesus, and Rome because they were often employed by Master Builders in the construction of churches, cathedrals, and basilicas.

Solsticial Rectangle of Ephesus

The connection with the sun is only one of the important features of Solsticial Rectangles. Our ancestors discovered other things happen when you mark the rectangle of the sun on the earth. A sacred space is created, and all the ancient cultures used this technique. The Christians used it because their building lineage followed the traditions and practices passed down from the Egyptians, Greeks, and Romans.

Solsticial Rectangle of Rome

Let's explore in detail what happens when a Solsticial Rectangle is built. First of all, there is a creation of a link between the earth and the sun. Next is the appearance of an energy vortex in the center, where none was before. A unique ambiance is generated inside, and the place becomes imbued with a special and healthy connection with life. Animals, trees, and plants recognize the shift in the energy of the space and connect with the central vortex, profiting from its new and exceptional power. A dome of energy protecting the entire structure appears around it.

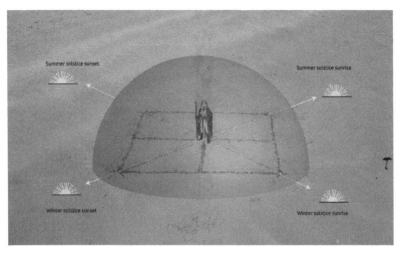

Dome of energy with energy vortex in the center of the structure

This solar structure needs to be strong and is dependent on the weight placed on the corners and sides. The more weight equals more reaction from the earth. When enough weight has been placed in the corners, huge energy streams appear in the NS and EW axes. Lastly, energetic doorways appear around the structure and the dome.

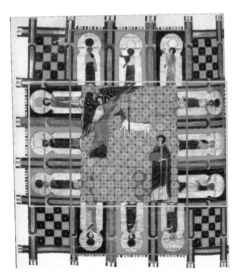

In the Christian tradition, there are 12 doorways. These energetic doors are found in the Celestial Jerusalem mythology and were illustrated in the Illuminated Manuscripts of the Beatus Codex during the 8th - 13th centuries. These illustrations used the Solsticial Rectangle of Jerusalem to create a link between their vision of Celestial Jerusalem and the Codex.

Beatus Codex of San Salvador Tábara, 10th century

For these reasons, the Solsticial Rectangle was (and still is) considered a unique sacred structure.

Of course, all the structures designed with this principle are sacred structures. Most of the religious temples and churches worldwide were designed and built with this remarkable Solsticial Rectangle as their foundation.

Our Neolithic ancestors worked very hard to build their megalithic stone monuments. The word megalith comes from the Greek words, mega - big and lithos - stone. Many of these megaliths marked the most important moments of the solar rhythm and the year. At Crucuno, Brittany, there is an extraordinary megalithic stone rectangle, built around 3000BC, which reproduces the solar rhythm of the place.

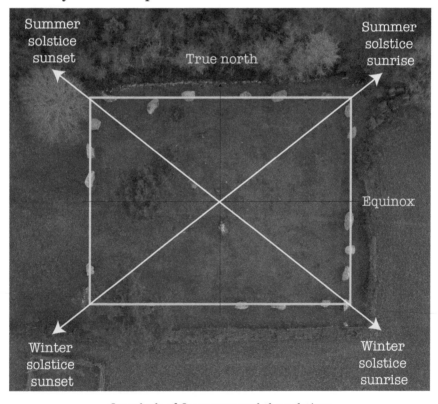

Cromlech of Cruncuno and the solstices

This Neolithic technique, which we call the Solsticial Rectangle, inaugurated a "technology" that continues to be applied in sacred construction today. Our Neolithic ancestors' invention is the beginning point for the mandala concept - a Hindu sacred space organization. In modern times, regulating lines use geometric proportions in buildings, giving them harmony and order stemming from the solar rhythm pattern. Crucuno is one example of this technology. Another is the Ziggurat of Ur Nammu, built by the Sumerians shown in the illustration below. The yellow rectangles depict how the Solsticial Rectangle was employed in the design of the Ziggurat.

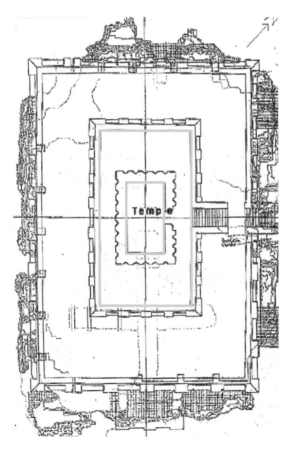

Ziggurat of Ur Nammu

The 5000-year old geometry of Crucuno is more complex than a simple rectangle of the sun. This Solsticial Rectangle is the classic figure from traditional Energetic Geometry called the 3:4 Rectangle. Deriving from the famous 3:4:5 Isis Triangle, it is probably much older than Crucuno itself. Master Builders have used it to draw right angles since the dawn of time. Later in this book, you will see it employed by the Master Builder of the Cathedral of St. Francis of Assisi.

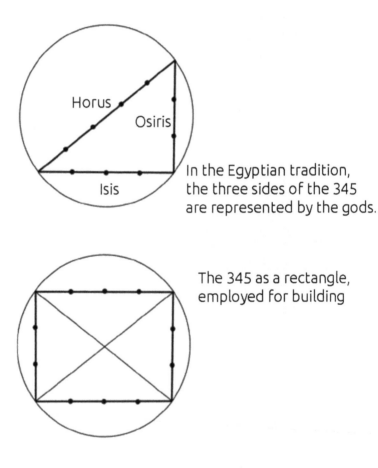

In the Egyptian tradition, the three sides of the 345 are represented by the gods.

The 345 as a rectangle, employed for building

The famous Isis 3:4:5 Rectangle

golden proportion

Most of us understand that the golden ratio is extraordinary. Still, when it comes to the mathematical reasons behind it, that's another thing. A straightforward definition is that two quantities are in the golden ratio if their ratio is the same as the ratio of their sum to the larger of the two quantities. It can be easier to understand by looking at the illustration of the golden ratio.

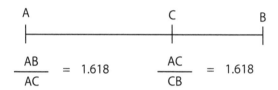

$$\frac{AB}{AC} = 1.618 \qquad \frac{AC}{CB} = 1.618$$

One important thing to note is that the Master Builders always used ratios in their designs, as you will see when we get to the analysis of the geometry employed in the churches.

The golden mean was used extensively by the European Master Builders. Its importance as the divine proportion is because

it is one of rhythms which preside over the development of all living things. It is found in DNA and in the development of plants and animals both at the micro and macro levels. When it is combined with solar geometry and utilized to build, it adds a rhythm necessary for the enhancement of life.

Spirals in nature

Master Builders employed the golden mean as a proportion found in ten Dynamic Rectangles. These special rectangles are connected to the golden mean through their proportion or sometimes through their angles and diagonals. Some of the Dynamic Rectangles have names like √5 Rectangle, the Parthenon Rectangle with its proportion of 1 ÷ 2.162 and the Cheops Rectangle with a 1 ÷ 1.272 proportion. Others are only represented by proportions such as 1 ÷ 1.376 or 1 ÷ 1.538.

There is an explanation of all the rectangles used by the Master Builders in Santa Fe in the Appendix.

master builder tradition in action

New Mexico has a long history with the Spanish and the Franciscan missionaries who accompanied them to build churches and spread their faith. We are fortunate to have some examples of the work of the European Master Builders in Santa Fe that span a few centuries, giving us a glimpse into the geometrical continuity of the tradition of building churches.

We will begin with the Mission of San Miguel because it is referred to as the oldest church in the United States. Next, is the Shrine of Our Lady of Guadalupe, which is the oldest shrine dedicated to Our Lady of Guadalupe still in use in the United States. The Cathedral of St. Francis of Assisi and the Loretto Chapel are both interesting examples of how the Master Builder tradition and techniques continued unbroken through the mid 19th century.

All four churches we researched in Santa Fe are similar in concept to many of the Romanesque churches and cathedrals built in France and Spain. Through our exploration of them, we will demonstrate how the energies of the earth are combined with the energy from the heavens to create well-balanced, powerful, spiritual healing spaces.

the importance of the location

The decision of where to place a church is a very important one. The healing energies of sacred structures are always underpinned by a subterranean network of water veins and geological faults. This technique of using earth energies, especially water, is found in all temples and churches around the world. In France, the Celts called these large underground water circulations "Vouivre." They are depicted as mythical serpents or dragons wearing a carbuncle on their forehead.

A Vouivre

In India, these underground water currents were called "Nagas." They were also called "Dragons" or "Tigers" in Imperial China by Feng Shui specialists. Subterranean water circulations can be huge, and some are over 10 meters wide. The strength and power of this type justify the term 'underground river.'

A Naga found in Bhutan
Photo credit: Karen Crowley-Susani

Below is a drawing of the energetic functioning of a crossing of water veins. It is important to note, that directly above these crossings, an energy vortex is generated. Depending on the place, the vortex generated has different strengths, colors, and overall tonalities.

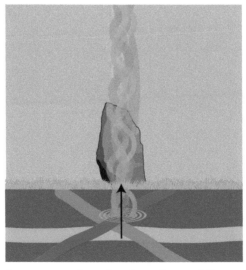

A stone placed over a crossing of water veins and the vortex of energy

These crossings of water veins circulating at different depths were much sought after by our ancestors. In Europe, they were used for building megaliths, such as menhirs, dolmens, and cromlechs. The example above depicts rivers of water flowing underneath a menhir. These types of water crossings were ideal locations to dig wells to supply water all year round, since two or more water veins fed them. There is a difference of potential between the two water veins.

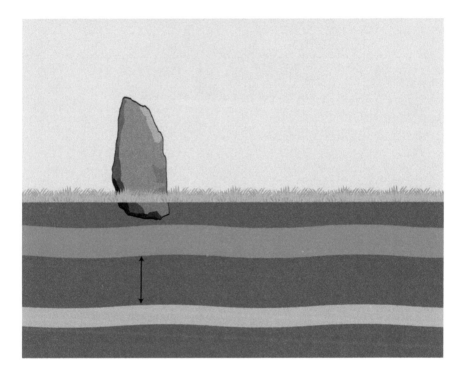

The difference of potential between the two water veins

In the Southwest, water veins were also used in the construction of kivas, wholly or partly underground religious chambers, and other sacred places of the Pueblo people. As can be seen in the illustration, the Aztec Kiva has a network of subterranean water veins and geological faults flowing below the structure. The central indigo vortex lends energy relating to the 3rd eye, perhaps indicating the kiva was used for vision quests.

The earth energies found at the Aztec Kiva in New Mexico
Earth energies drawing by Nicolas Susani

building a sacred place

Building a sacred place was a lengthy process. After choosing the site, the surrounding area around was leveled. A gnomon was placed in the center, representing the axis of the world, the Axis Mundi.

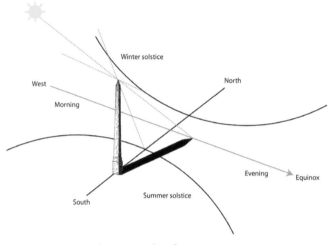

An example of a gnomon

This was followed by a long period of observation of the equinoxes and solstices. Observation of the equinoxes was essential in order to mark the cardinal directions. In the tradition of the Master Builders, the east west direction is the axis of the Mother (Mother Earth). The observation of the shadow of the equinoxes with the gnomon is quite simple. Because there are two equinoxes, the shadows repeat in the spring and autumn. This repetition allows for the determination of east/west direction with excellent accuracy (0.005%). From this initial point, the remainder of the cardinal directions are easy to determine.

According to the 5th century Hindu book of Vastuśāstra, Mayamata, a method known to the Hindus for millennia, is called the fish figure. Once these four directions were in place, the tracing of the solar rhythm of the site could begin.

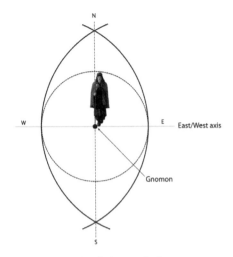

The fish symbol

The Master Builder usually made the observations during the summer solstice because the skies were often clear around this time, making it easier to observe the sunrise on the horizon. Traditionally, the marking ritual was made when the solar corona was halfway above the horizon, as shown in the drawing.

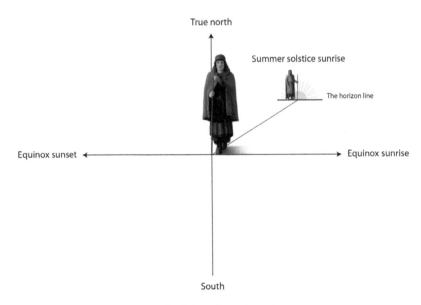

Master Builder observing the sun

Master Builders knew from antiquity that the angles of the summer solstice sunrise and the winter solstice sunrise were the same. This figure became a symbol called the Goosefoot. At the church of San Martín de Fromísta in Spain, there is a goosefoot symbol found between the two Templar crosses.

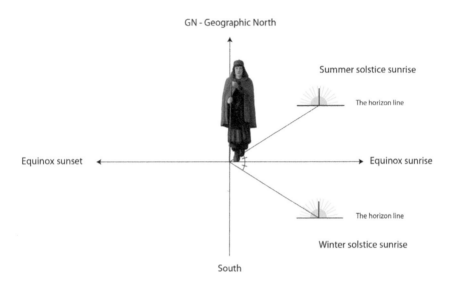

The goosefoot symbol at the church of San Martín de Fromísta

These same angles are then drawn for the solstice sunsets. As you can see in the drawing, when connected together with parallel lines, a rectangular form emerges, called the Solsticial Rectangle.

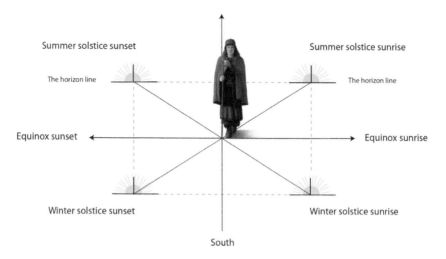

The Master Builder inside the Solsticial Rectangle

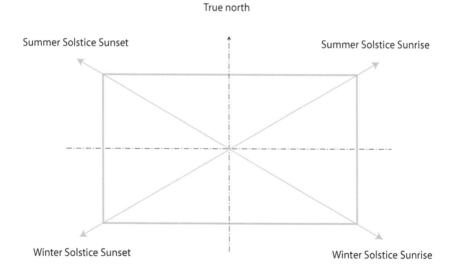

The Solsticial Rectangle of Santa Fe in the 17th century

Once the Master Builder had drawn the Solsticial Rectangle, he squared it by duplicating the rectangle in the north-south direction. This new rectangle is called the Lunar Rectangle for two reasons. The first, is that this north/south-oriented rectangle is subtle in feeling and has a strong tendency to act on the psyche like the energy of the moon.

The second reason is that at certain latitudes, this Lunar Rectangle's energetic solar geometry corresponds with the extreme positions of the moon in the Meton cycle. This phenomenon occurs at the latitude of Stonehenge, as demonstrated in the studies of astronomer, Dr. Gerald Hawkins, who wrote about it in his books, *Stonehenge Decoded* (Doubleday 1965) and *Beyond Stonehenge* (Harper 1975).

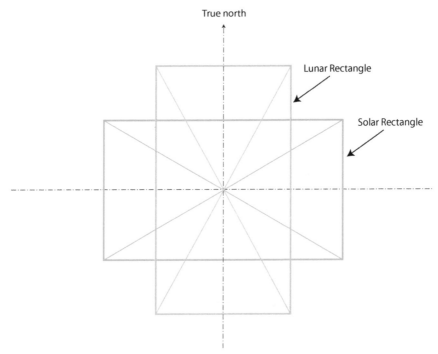

The geometry of the Lunar Rectangle

When both the Solar (Sosticial) and Lunar Rectangles are in place, we can draw a square to enclose the two rectangles, which is called the Mother Square.

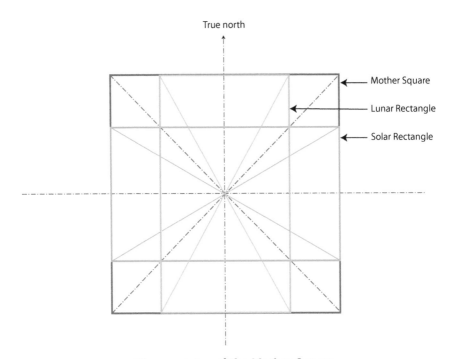

The geometry of the Mother Square

From the Mother Square, the mandala of the place begins to unfold, making it possible to find the measurements of the five elements, Earth, Water, Fire, Air, and Ether of the place.

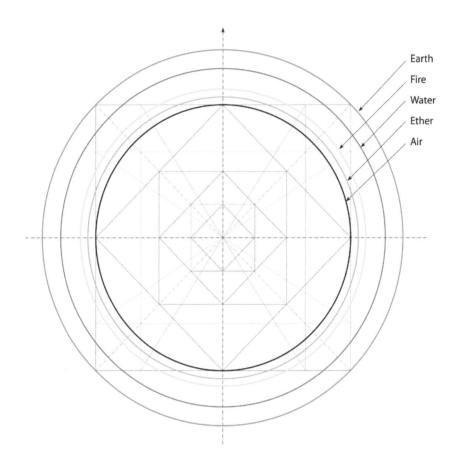

The geometry of the elements within the solar mandala

Chapter Two

history of the mission of san miguel

The Mission of San Miguel
Photo credit: Karen Crowley-Susani

The Mission of San Miguel was built around 1610, shortly after the founding of Santa Fe. The Franciscan missionaries who were directly involved in building churches and missions in the Southwest oversaw the building of the Mission of San Miguel. The labor was probably provided by the Tlaxcalan Indians, who accompanied the Spaniards from Mexico. They lived among the Pueblo natives in the Barrio de Analco on the left bank of the Santa Fe River. Because missionary work was a priority for the Spanish, they built the Mission of San Miguel to serve this native population before building their own parish church. Its purpose was to be a mission for the natives, whom the Spanish had converted, and the various Indian groups accompanying the Spanish from Mexico.

Inside of the Mission of San Miguel
Photo credit: Karen Crowley-Susani

San Miguel was first mentioned in writing in 1628, and the original church was probably smaller than the present structure. It was described as having a rectangular apse, a simple facade with no towers, and a slightly raised sanctuary or shrine.

The history of San Miguel is fraught with power struggles between church and state, as well as uprisings from the Puebloan people. In 1640, during a Spanish battle for power, Governor Luis de Rosas had San Miguel torn down to thwart the Franciscan friars. Then, in 1680 during the Pueblo Revolt, the church was burned down by the Pueblo people.

Even though the church walls remained after the fire, it wasn't until after Diego de Vargas led the Spanish back to Santa Fe in 1692, that the Franciscans could quickly rebuild their church.

In 1710, Marqués de la Peñuela bought the governorship of New Mexico and began the rebuilding process with the blessings of Admiral Don José Chacón Medina Salazar y Villaseñor. To raise funds for the rebuilding, the statue of St. Michael went on tour throughout the colony. Master Builder Andrés González, a 60 year old native of Zacatecas, Mexico, oversaw the rebuilding project. The church was probably built on the same foundations, and the original rectangular apse changed to a trapezoid.

The bell tower which was added to the front of the church sometime in the 1830s, collapsed in 1872. The structure continued to decline until the Christian Brothers bought the church and rebuilt the bell tower and stabilized the walls in 1887. It was remodeled into its current form in 1955.

Three other interesting components of the church include the statue of St. Michael, the wooden altar reredos, (an ornamental wall screen behind the altar) and the bell. The statue of St. Michael sits inside the center niche of the reredos and dates back to 1709. It originated in Mexico and was brought to New Mexico by the Franciscan Friars, and has been a part of the

The Statue of San Miguel
Photo credit: Karen Crowley-Susani

church since at least 1776.

In the 1790s, a painted wooden reredos was commissioned and installed by Antonio José Ortiz, a patron of the church. The 22 foot altar screen was most likely created by New Mexico's anonymous "Laguna Santero" who was active in New Mexico between 1796 and 1808. It was dated by the artist in 1798. At the top center is an image of Archangel Michael, painted in 1745 by Bernardo de Miera y Pacheco. Below Archangel Michael is a painting of Christ, dating back to the mid 1800s and oil paintings on each side dating to the early 1800s. Clockwise from top to left, St. Teresa of Ávila, St. Gertrude, St. Louis, and St. Francis of Assisi are depicted. To either side of the carved Archangel Michael are two unidentified saints dating back to the 19th century.

The Reredos inside the Mission of San Miguel
Photo Credit: Karen Crowley-Susani

The bell, which now rests in the church, had hung in the bell tower before its collapse in 1872. It has been a source of mystery and legends because of its age and was believed to have come from Spain. It had an unlikely date of 1356, which was debunked in 1914 by Benjamin Read, who located a local man who remembered it being cast in Santa Fe in 1856.

The bell inside the Mission of San Miguel
Photo Credit: Karen Crowley-Susani

analysis of subterranean influences

San Miguel was constructed using a classic configuration of subterranean influences, well-known by the Master Builders. The strategy of the Spanish for the conversion of the native population in the Americas consisted of occupying their sacred places. It is very well known that they built the Cathedral of Mexico City over the Aztecan Temple Mayor. In the case of San Miguel, a story that we were told during our investigations was that the altar was built over a kiva. Unfortunately, we found no evidence to support this theory. What can be seen, however, is the altar was built over an Indian dwelling dating back to 1300. In the altar area there are three plexiglass windows showing the stairs and dwelling below.

One of the plexiglass windows showing the stairs and dwelling below.
Photo credit: Karen Crowley-Susani

Subterranean energies of the place are very important in building a sacred structure, and for San Miguel they play a very important part.

In the drawing, you can see several types of energies. The thick blue lines represent water veins. The red lines represent geological faults and the colored circles are vortexes of energy found on the surface of the earth. The colors correspond to the chakra system of the body. In ascending order from the root to the crown chakra, they are red, orange, yellow, green, light blue, indigo, and violet.

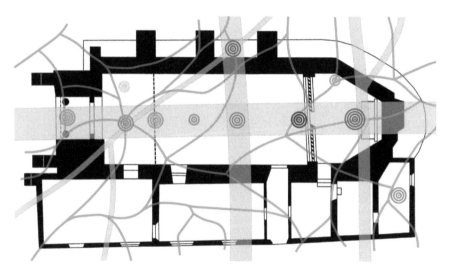

The subterranean earth energies of San Miguel
Earth energies drawing by Nicolas Susani

In San Miguel, the subterranean water veins are a classic configuration for a normal church. There is one large central water vein flowing east/west direction with several others crossing it. The width of the main water vein is fairly large, so people walking down the central aisle are walking over the water vein. This is interesting because there is an exchange of information between the place and people who enter into the church.

Water assists people in receiving the information of sacred places. It should be understood, that water covers everything on the surface of the earth. To give a little clarity to this idea, all the humidity in our air is water in the form of steam. Just like air is everywhere, water is too. The humidity or steam in the air varies, for example, in Santa Fe, the humidity averages 32% .

Because of this fact, the air of a church or cathedral is informed by the vibration created by the structure, the geometry, and surface energies such as vortexes. This is why a special ambiance is found in sacred places and people are able to access a deeper spiritual connection there. The solar geometry, together with geometry connected to the golden mean, create a place full of life force energy thanks to water and air.

In San Miguel, people benefit from the peaceful and regenerating violet ambiance. The vibration of rituals and Mass, also contribute to the energy found inside. Because of this special energetic ambiance, people often enjoy spending time within churches.

To continue with the subterranean energies of San Miguel, the two water veins which cross at the apse, generate a powerful violet vortex. Usually, churches dedicated to St. Michael have a golden vortex, but here the violet tonality is a spiritual and healing energy connected with the 7th chakra. This violet energy facilitates a connection with the heavens.

The two water crossings near the middle of the nave have a clear blue vortex of energy. This vortex opens the 5th chakra, the throat chakra. The last water crossing at the beginning of the nave, defined with the crossing of many geological faults, is a red vortex connected to the 1st chakra. This red vortex helps those entering the church experience being fully grounded, which is an essential component of a spiritual life.

San Miguel has a good chakra path. This energetic pathway is found in all temples and churches. Chakra paths are associated with the seven main chakras of the human body. Walking along this energetic pathway in a church allows the chakra system to open and balance, resulting in feeling a deeper connection to the Mass and communion. For example, walking from the west along the chakra path, your energy and vibration rise and as you arrive before the altar you are energetically prepared for the spiritual experience of communion.

analysis of the geometry of the place

Historically, the apse is the first part of the church to be built. There are several reasons why. Firstly, it is the place in the church where the highest vibrational energy is found. Secondly, after the sacred space of the apse was built, the priest would have a structure where Mass could be conducted while the rest of the church was being built.

An important tradition that the Master Builders employed was using a polygon which matched the location's solar mandala. These are special polygons that naturally connect to the sun at specific latitudes. In Santa Fe, there are two of these special polygons. One is the hexagon, the polygon of six. As you can see in the illustration below, the short side of the Solsticial Rectangle equals one side of the hexagon.

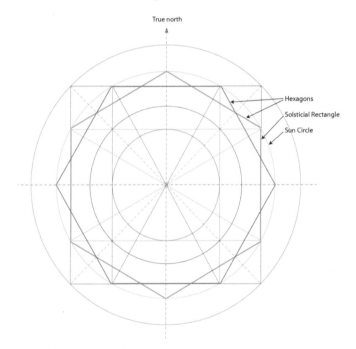

The hexagon in the solar mandala of Santa Fe

The other polygon is the pentagon. This polygon of five is important because it circumscribes the Sun Circle, as seen in the drawing below. The Sun Circle is the circle that touches the corners of the Solsticial Rectangle. The pentagon is connected to the golden mean and the element of Fire.

The pentagon was a very famous and well-known geometric figure in antiquity. In the 4th century, Plato linked the pentagon to the dodecahedron and the element of Ether. Other Greek mathematicians, such as Euclid, studied the pentagon and its relationship with the golden ratio.

The Master Builder of San Miguel was aware of the relationship that these two polygons had with the sun in the solar mandala of Santa Fe, and used them in the design of San Miguel.

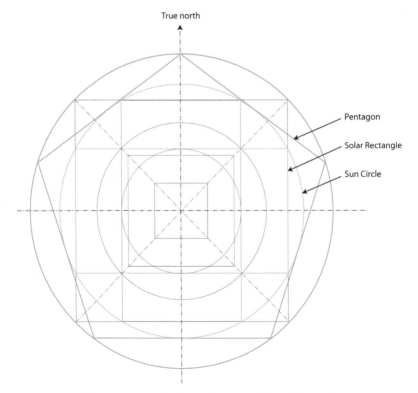

The pentagon in the solar mandala of Santa Fe

The main energetical point of the apse of San Miguel is the crossing of the two water veins and the violet vortex. It is the beginning point of the first construction. The hexagon was used to design the apse, and as can be seen in the illustration, the three inner sides of the apse are found by tracing the hexagon around the Sun Circle.

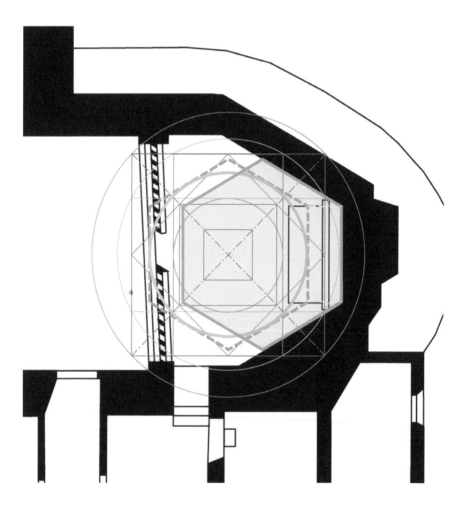

The use of the hexagon in the apse of San Miguel

Another hexagon can be traced using the side of the Solsticial Rectangle as one of its sides, shown in green. It is found by multiplying the first hexagon by √2 or by 1.414. This hexagon determines the limits of sacred space materialized by the wooden reredos altar screen. This hexagon is also inscribed within a solar circle. Connected to the element of Ether, it imbues the altar with energy full of life force, peace and opens the heart. Also, note how this hexagon was used to determine the limits of the trapezoidal apse.

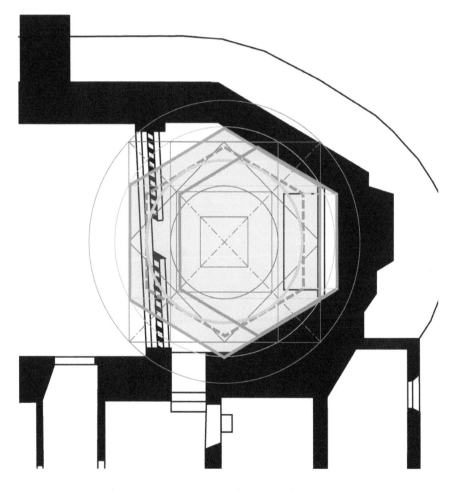

The second hexagon in the apse of San Miguel

To find the thickness of the walls, the Master Builder multiplied the 2nd hexagon by √2, as seen in the illustration below. This hexagon is connected to the element of Earth which lends the energy of strength and solidness to the apse.

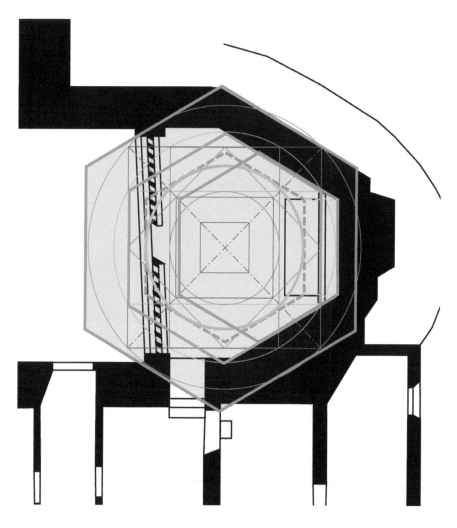

The third hexagon in the apse of San Miguel

the nave

For the width of the nave's interior, the Master Builder of San Miguel used the Sun Circle and the other natural polygon of Santa Fe, the pentagon. The diameter of the sun circle fits within 1.5% of the current width of the nave, which is a small percentage given the rebuilding history of the church.

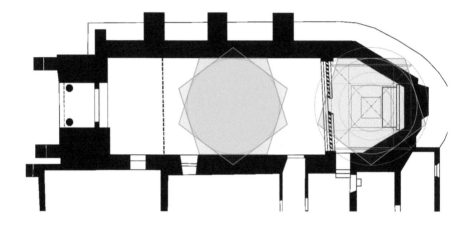

The pentagon and the nave of San Miguel

In the tradition of the Master Builders, Dynamic Rectangles were employed for specific measurements. Dynamic Rectangles have a direct relationship with the golden ratio. This relationship can be hidden because it is related to the ratio of the diagonals or half diagonals. One of these Dynamic Rectangles that the Master Builder used is a proportion related to the golden mean of $1 \div 2.752$.

This gives the length of the entire nave. It also connects the nave to the trapezoidal apse shown in the illustration on the next page.

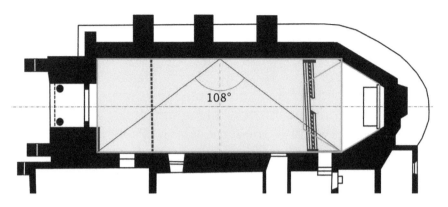

The Divine Delta and Dynamic Rectangle of 1 ÷ 2.752

When this remarkable rectangle is divided by two, we obtain two rectangles called the 1.376 Rectangle. Which was an important measurement used by artists in the Renaissance. This particular rectangle of 1 ÷ 2.752 is also connected with the Divine Delta Triangle with its sublime angle of 108°. It was a secret reminder of musical notes and proportions in the geometry of the place.

The nave has another Dynamic Rectangle associated with it called the √5 Rectangle. This exceptional rectangle was well-known, widely used, and has a special solar relationship with Santa Fe. As we shall see, each church in Santa Fe uses this √5 Rectangle somewhere in its design. It was because of the remarkable ability of four Solsticial Rectangles of Santa Fe to fit precisely inside this √5 Rectangle.

This Dynamic Rectangle is most connected to the golden mean, and the mix between the √5 Rectangle and the four Solsticial Rectangles has two aspects. The first is that the combination between the two makes the structure fully connected to life force energy, and enhances the power of the form itself. This makes the vibration inside faster and higher, and of course, more spiritual. Another essential aspect is the type of Element the short side of the √5 Rectangle embodies. In San Miguel, the Element of the short side is Cosmic Fire. It is directly related to the pentagon and the Sun Circle, producing a feeling of elevation that spreads information throughout the church, and cleaning the energies of the people inside.

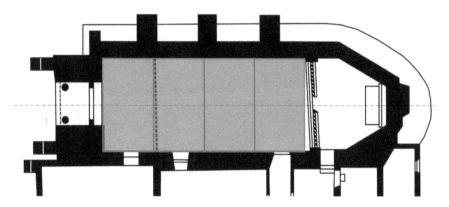

The √5 Rectangle with the four Solsticial Rectangles of Santa Fe inside

Next, the thickness of the walls is found by using the √5 Rectangle and a Double Square Rectangle, as seen in the following two illustrations. These two rectangles have the same width giving us the dimensions of the narthex and the nave.

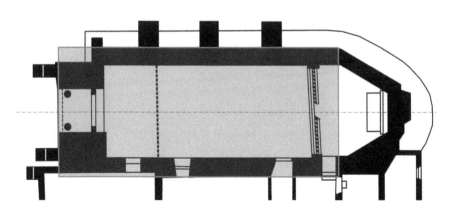

The √5 Rectangle

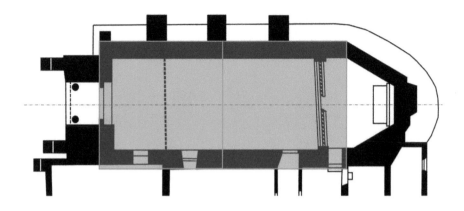

Double Square Rectangle

Lastly, two Solsticial Rectangles envelop the church; Santa Fe as seen below and Jerusalem, on the next page.

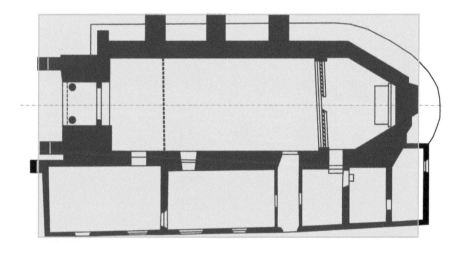

Solsticial Rectangle of Santa Fe

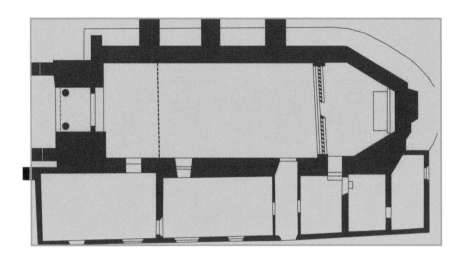

Solsticial Rectangle of Jerusalem

conclusion

Looking even more closely at the building concept of the Mission of San Miguel, it was designed with logic and the geometric tools of the European Master Builders for two main reasons. The first is the Master Builder, who designed San Miguel possessed the knowledge, skill, and tools consistent with the European history of church and cathedral building.

Second, various modifications to the church through the centuries were made by professionals who were initiated in sacred construction and solar geometry used by the Master Builders. For example, the knowledge of the hexagon and its relationship to the sun was known. During rebuilding of the church in the 18th century, the rectangular apse was redesigned by Master Builder Gonzales, who employed a hexagon, making the energies of this sacred place stronger and more consistent with the solar mandala of Santa Fe.

Also, during the last renovation and the addition of buttresses, the overall rectangular envelope around the church has the proportions of the Solsticial Rectangle of Jerusalem, a common technique used by the Master Builders to connect the church to the Holy Land, and therefore, to Christ.

Chapter Three

history of the shrine of our lady of guadalupe

The Shrine of Our Lady of Guadalupe
Photo credit: Ayla Angela

Interior of the Shrine of Our Lady of Guadalupe
Photo credit: Ayla Angelo

The Sanctuario de Nuestra Señora de Guadalupe is the oldest standing church dedicated to Our Lady of Guadalupe in the United States. The date of the original adobe church is a mystery, with some saying it was built between 1776 and 1795, but there is no recorded evidence until 1821.

It was a place of worship built close the end of El Camino Real. The old royal highway linked settlers, traders, and soldiers traveling from Mexico up through Veracruz, Mexico City, Chihuahua, El Paso, Socorro, Albuquerque to Santa Fe. Many of these people settled on the banks of the Santa Fe River. They were devoted to Our Lady of Guadalupe, and a shrine dedicated to her was built to accommodate their needs.

The first, was a tiny adobe church which went through many changes during the centuries. The roof style and the position of the bell tower changed according to the fashion through the years. The shrine was restored around 1887, and in 1920, it was remodeled into its current form in 1976. The Shrine of Our Lady of Guadalupe is now a small museum of art and history.

On the altar screen, the reredos, is Our Lady of Guadalupe's most prominent and best oil painting in the Spanish Southwest. Four illustrations of the main events of the visitation of Mary to Juan Diego surround it. Renowned Mexican artist José de Alzibar painted it in 1783. It traveled north in sections by covered wagons along El Camino Real.

The altar and reredos of the Shrine of Our Lady of Guadalupe
Photo credit: Ayla Angelo

The history of the cult of Our Lady of Guadalupe began in Mexico when Mary appeared to newly converted Aztecan peasant, Juan Diego in 1531, near present-day Mexico City. She was dark-skinned, spoke in his native language, and requested a shrine be built on Tepeyac hill. The Bishop demanded a sign before he approved the construction of a church. Mary appeared again to Juan Diego and told him to gather flowers from the top of the hill. It was December, and flowers were not in season, but he did as he was instructed. He found non-native Castilian roses blooming on top of the barren hill.

Mary helped him arrange them inside his cloak, called a tilma so that he could take them to the Bishop as evidence. Juan showed the flowers to the Bishop and to their amazement, there was a life-size image of the Virgin Mary on the inside of the tilma.

Our Lady of Guadalupe
Photo credit: Ayla Angelo

analysis of subterranean influences

Guadalupe is a sanctuary church with a pilgrimage dedicated to Our Lady of Guadalupe. The basic shape of the church is a traditional Latin cross with an apse, transept, and nave. The earth energies employed to build it are classic. The main water vein runs down the central aisle with several crossings. The main intersection of water veins is located at the central point of the transept. This crossing generates a powerful, clear blue vortex connected to the throat chakra, allowing the devotees to open to greater spirituality.

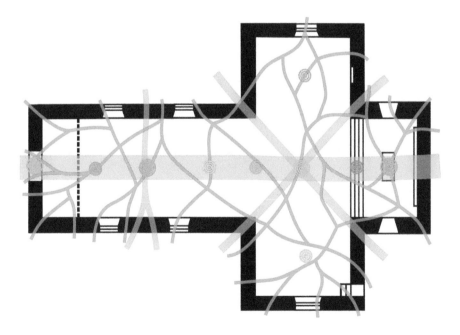

The subterranean influences of the Shrine of Our Lady of Guadalupe
Earth energies drawing by Nicolas Susani

Fertility waters are used in many churches dedicated to Mary. Here, it is found in the nave as a water crossing generating a strong vortex connected to the second chakra.

Another characteristic associated with Marian churches is the energy of love and the opening of the heart chakra. The powerful green vortex at the entrance of the shrine helps to open people's hearts as they enter.

The rainbow-colored chakra path running the length of the church begins at the door with the opening of the heart. It continues with the first chakra, and rises through all the chakras in a very regular pattern. It is connected geometrically with the seven Solsticial Rectangles that make up the entire length of the church ending with a strong violet vortex in the center of the apse. On the left side of the transept is a healing crystalline vortex that can clean the body's central channel.

analysis of the geometry of the place

The external shape of the Sanctuario de Nuestra Señora de Guadalupe consists of three remarkable rectangles which are very well-known in the tradition of the European Master Builders. The first one depicted in red enclosing the apse is the Solsticial Rectangle of Jerusalem. This rectangle was classically used to connect the place to the Christ energy associated with Jerusalem. The second rectangle in the transept is violet and is the famous √5 Rectangle. It is an extraordinary shape because four Solsticial Rectangles of Santa Fe fit exactly inside, making it a potent form for the place. The characteristics of the √5 Rectangle were touched upon at the Mission of San Miguel. The third rectangle depicted in blue is a classic rectangle found in sites dedicated to the Virgin. Ephesus is where Mary is believed to have lived out her last days. The ratio of the Ephesus Rectangle was used to connect churches to Mother Mary.

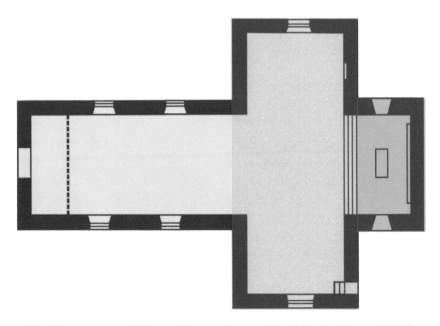

The three exterior Solsticial Rectangles employed by the Master Builder

The interior of the apse uses a Solsticial Rectangle of Santa Fe for maximum power, and to enhance the strength of the violet vortex found at the center. Violet vortexes were often used for the apse because they open the crown chakra and link to greater spirituality.

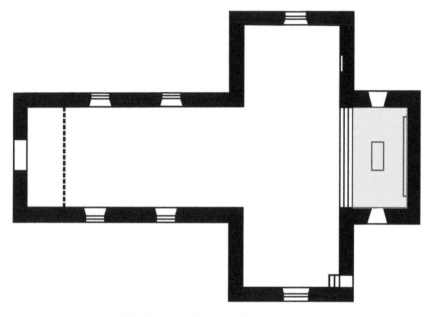

The Solsticial Rectangle of the apse

The entire inner transept is made with the Dynamic Rectangle, Φ^2. (1.618 x 1.618 = 2.618) This rectangle has a ratio of 1 ÷ 2.618 and is one of the Golden Mean Rectangles. When a square is drawn in the center of this rectangle, another unique form emerges. The two sides, depicted in green, have the Cheops Pyramid Rectangle measurements of 1 ÷ 1.272, another famous Dynamic Rectangle used by the Master Builders.

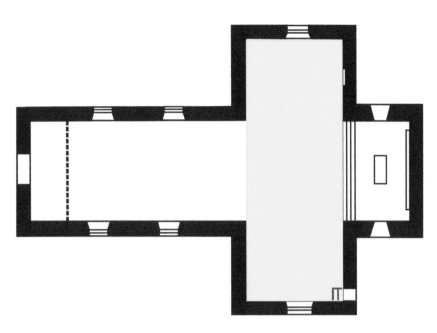

The interior transept with the Golden Mean Rectangle of 1 ÷ 2.618

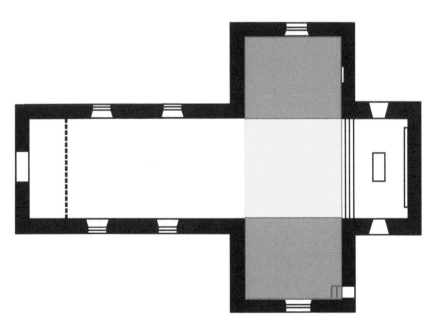

The two Cheops Pyramid Rectangles inside the transept

55

The Master Builder employed the √5 Rectangle again for the measurement of the nave's interior, giving it good energetic strength. The four Solsticial Rectangles of Santa Fe can be found within this rectangle, but the architect did something else with these rectangles; he used exactly seven Solsticial Rectangles of Santa Fe for the entire length of the interior, empowering the whole church.

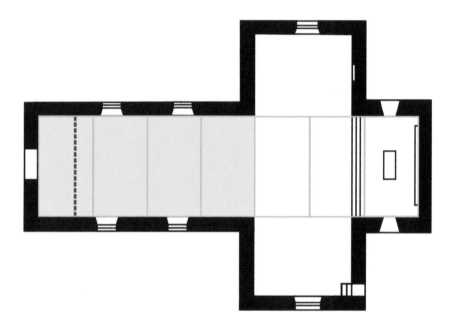

The Solsticial Rectangles of the nave

conclusion

In conclusion, we can say that the geometry of the Shrine of
Our Lady of Guadalupe is a masterpiece of the art of the Master
Builders. Technically, the architect profoundly understood the
energetic patterns of Santa Fe, and created a church using the
best geometry that the solar mandala of Santa Fe could offer.
He combined the knowledge of how to mix the earth energies
with the geometry of the place to create a powerful and sacred
healing sanctuary.

Our Lady of Guadalupe
Photo credit: Ayla Angelo

Chapter Four

history of the cathedral of st. francis of assisi

Cathedral of St. Francis of Assisi
Photo credit: Kingjon from Canstock photos

The Cathedral of St. Francis, like the Mission of San Miguel, has a long history of unrest, revolts, and rebuilding. The first parish church was built around 1610, rebuilt in 1630, and burned down and destroyed during the Pueblo revolt of 1680. The church was not rebuilt again until 1714, but this time in a new place that faced the plaza. The tiny Chapel of the Conquistadora was built off the north arm of the transept. After some time, the parish church collapsed, and it too, was rebuilt again around 1804. Another chapel dedicated to San José was added to the southern transept.

Interior of St. Francis
Photo Credit: Ayla Angelo

These renovations were made possible by the generous church benefactor, Don Antonio José Ortiz, a leading member of the active religious society in Santa Fe. St. Francis needed constant renovations because it was an adobe structure and didn't age well. It became a cathedral, but even though it was big for an adobe church, it still lacked the light and spiritual nature of a European cathedral.

The rebuilding of St. Francis began again in 1869 through the vision of the first Bishop, Father John Baptiste Lamy of France. He decided that the old adobe church of 1714 was inadequate for the seat of the Archdiocese, and ordered a new Romanesque cathedral to be built instead. After seeing the ineptness of the Anglo architect, he employed French architects, Antoine Mouly and his son Projectus, along with Italian stonemasons to rebuild the church. The Moulys were also commissioned to build the Loretto Chapel for the Order of the Sisters of Loretto. The cathedral was built in stone, and the stained-glass windows were created in France and traveled to Santa Fe by ship and covered wagon. The new cathedral was built around the old parish church. It included the Chapel of the Conquistadora. In 1895 the Cathedral of St. Francis was finally consecrated.

The Spanish often brought Virgin Mary statues with them on their travels around the world. One of the most beloved statues associated with St. Francis is La Conquistadora, Our Lady of Peace or Our Lady of Conquering Love. She was the first Madonna brought to the United States. La Conquistadora was brought to Santa Fe by the priest Fray Alonso de Benavides from Mexico City in 1626.

There is a long history of armies carrying statues of gods and saints into battle. For example, the Black Madonna of Rocamadour was brought to the battle of Navas, in Tolosa in 1212, by the Knights of Rocamadour. La Conquistadora was no stranger to fighting either. She helped the Spanish during their reconquest of Santa Fe and the surrounding area 12 years after

The Chapel of the Conquistadora
Photo credit: Ayla Angelo

the Pueblo Revolt. Don Diego de Vargas hoped that she would aid in taking back the lands in a relatively bloodless manner. After returning to Santa Fe in 1693, a new tradition called the Fiesta of Santa Fe was held annually to celebrate and give thanks. It is the oldest Marian festival in the US and is still celebrated today.

Most churches and cathedrals have a large water vein running roughly east-west down the nave, as seen in churches of San Miguel and Our Lady of Guadalupe. This tradition is not the case in the cathedral of St. Francis. We don't know the motivation behind the choices made by the builders of St. Francis in regards to using or not using the standard subterranean energies. Maybe it was because the church immediately preceding the present cathedral was already there. Traditionally, bishops and the Master Builders used the same footprint of the original church. It was commonplace to either add to the existing church or completely rebuild it in the exact location. For example, the newest cathedral was built in Chartres using the same footprint as the five preceding churches.

The very first parish church of St. Francis was built in a different place and was located behind the current one. Its exact location is unknown, but perhaps this first church was placed over the traditional water vein configuration. However, it is not a question we can answer.

We can say that the subterranean energies of the apse of St. Francis have a classic type of configuration. It consists of a couple of water veins mixed with a geological fault that cross the center of the apse. Traditionally, the apse of a church has a violet point relating to the opening of the 7th chakra. But, the Master Builder chose a golden energy point instead. Golden energy points are typically associated with churches dedicated to St. Michael.

The Master Builder mixed the geometry of the golden mean with the golden point in the apse. Golden vortexes are healing vortexes, and when combined with the golden mean, the healing quality of the golden point is enhanced.

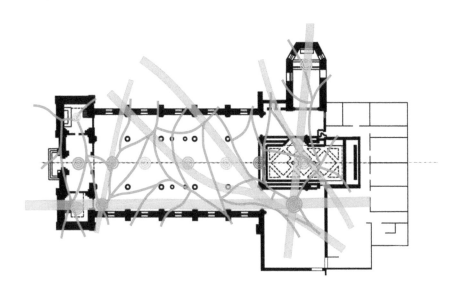

Subterranean earth energies of St. Francis of Assisi
Earth Energies drawing by Nicolas Susani

The energies of the nave have a good chakra path down the center. At the entrance of the apse, there is an indigo point, generated more by the geometry than by earth energies. The larger violet vortex generated by the water veins is an actual earth energy point traditionally used for the altar. Perhaps the old church of San Jose used this excellent point for its altar.

Lastly, the Conquistadora chapel has an excellent light blue vortex connected with the 5th chakra. The fifth chakra is called the door to spirituality because the upper chakras can be accessed more easily when this chakra is open.

analysis of the geometry of the place

The Cathedral of St. Francis of Assisi has a more elaborate design than San Miguel. It has the shape of a small cathedral, but its design is not as complex as ones found in Europe, mainly because of the lack of funds. However, the geometry applied to create the cathedral is worthy of an actual European-built cathedral. The Master Builder worked with Dynamic Rectangles and the golden mean in his design, like San Miguel. But his use of Dynamic Rectangles was more sophisticated, and contained many layers, as you will see in the analysis.

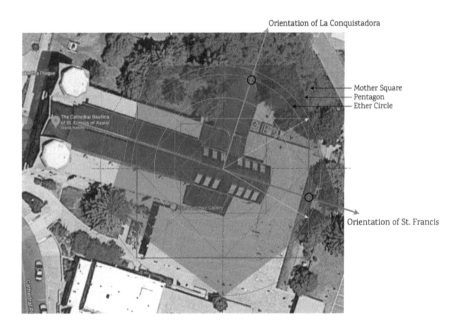

Orientation of St. Francis of Assisi

orientation

The first thing to notice about the St. Francis cathedral is the orientation. The Master Builder architect, Mouly, used the same orientation as the previous Spanish Master Builder, and is a classic European Romanesque church orientation. One aspect is the axis of the church which passes through the intersection of the Ether Circle and the side of the Mother Square. Next, the Master Builder tried to employ the natural polygon of the place in his design as much as possible. As you may recall, one characteristic of the solar mandala of Santa Fe is the pentagon.

As you can see in the illustration, the orientation of the cathedral corresponds to one of the pentagon points. The Chapel of our Lady of Conquistadora also connects the Santa Fe pentagon because it is tilted 90° off the orientation of St Francis. Because the direction of the La Conquistadora is to the north, it has energetic spiritual qualities. The energy is lighter and more connected to the psyche, so this orientation is referred to as lunar. The energetic quality of direction of St. Francis is stronger because it is connected with the axis of the Mother, and more associated with matter and the physical.

Orienting a church to the pentagon is known as an orientation of power. The pentagon is related to the element of Fire, and it can spread information. In this instance, during Mass or other rituals performed in the church, the information of the ceremony expands outwards. It is estimated that this influence has a radius of influence of up to 20 miles for a structure the size of a cathedral.

geometry of the nave

The nave begins with the basic measurement of the Solsticial Rectangle of Santa Fe and rapidly becomes increasingly complex. The Master Builder began working with the golden mean in the form of Dynamic Rectangles, starting with the √5 Rectangle.

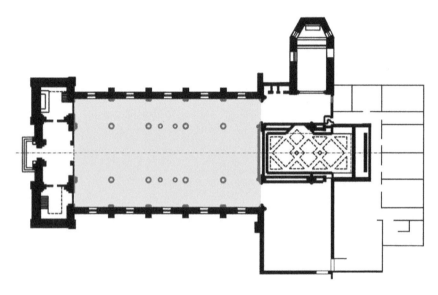

The nave and the Solsticial Rectangle of Santa Fe

This Dynamic Rectangle envelops the entire church from the narthex to the end of the apse. As seen before with San Miguel and Our Lady of Guadalupe, precisely four Solsticial Rectangles of Santa Fe fit inside this √5 Rectangle and are characteristic of Santa Fe's solar geometry. Using this technique is not possible at every latitude, but works very well in Santa Fe.

Next, the measurements of the narthex are found by dividing the Solsticial Rectangle of Santa Fe into four, as you can see in the drawing. Two of these were used for this measurements.

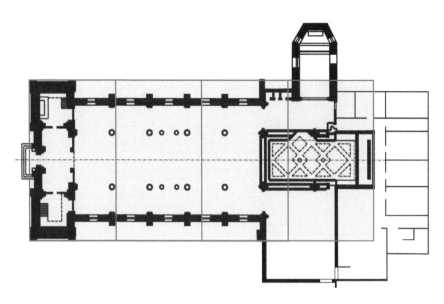

The √5 Rectangle with the four Solsticial Rectangles of Santa Fe inside

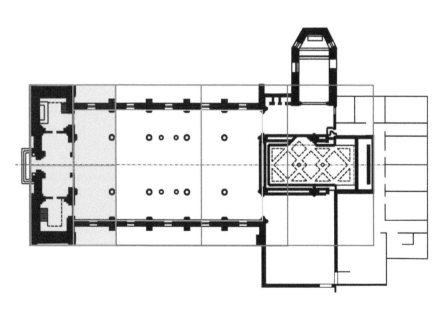

The measurement of the narthex is found by dividing the Solsticial Rectangle of Santa Fe into four

In the center of the nave, you can see how the columns were conceptualized. Down the middle are five Dynamic Rectangles of 1 ÷ 1.376, also called the 54/36 Rectangle. The name of this Dynamic Rectangle comes from the angles made by the diagonal, which are 54° and 36°. It is related to the golden mean by its proportions and diagonals and was used by Italian, Dutch, and French artists in their paintings during the Renaissance.

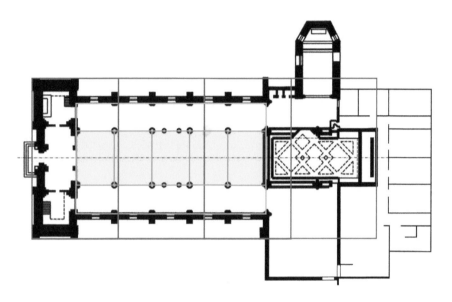

The position of the five Dynamic Rectangles in the nave

On either side of the center of the nave are five 3x4 Rectangles. They also give measurement and rhythm to the columns.

Next, is the complicated layering of sacred geometry found in the measurements of the columns. Beginning upon entering the nave, Mouly used two Double Square Rectangles depicted in blue.

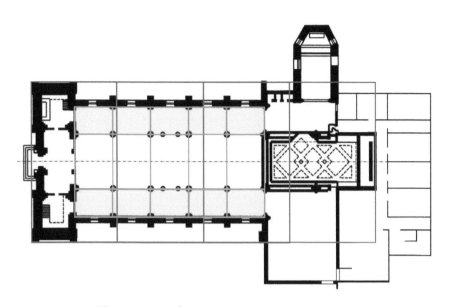

The position of the 3x4 Rectangles in the nave

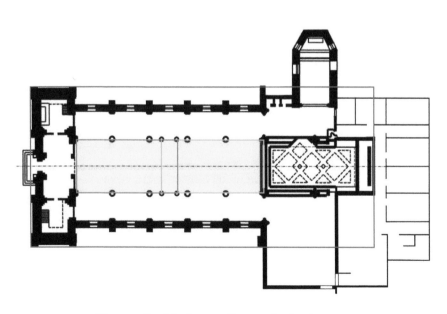

The two Double Square Rectangles in the nave

In the center, there are four smaller columns. Here, the Master Builder used a common technique of linking the cathedral to Jerusalem, an important spiritual place for Christians. The method of using the ratios of the Solsticial Rectangles of Jerusalem 1 ÷ 1.88, Rome 1 ÷ 1.57, and Ephesus 1 ÷ 1.70 were often employed by the Master Builders.

Using these ratios facilitated several things for the Christians. Jerusalem was the link to Christ and the foundation of Christianity. Rome was the link to the Pope and the Catholic Church, and Ephesus provided the link to the Virgin Mary.

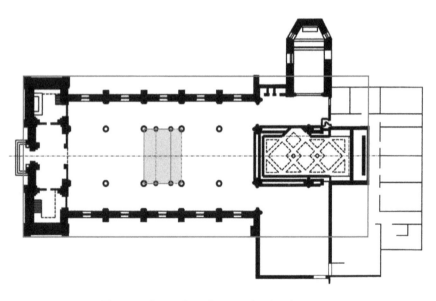

The two Jerusalem Rectangles in the nave

The last layer of sacred geometry connected to the columns are the two Golden Mean Rectangles shown in the illustration on the next page.

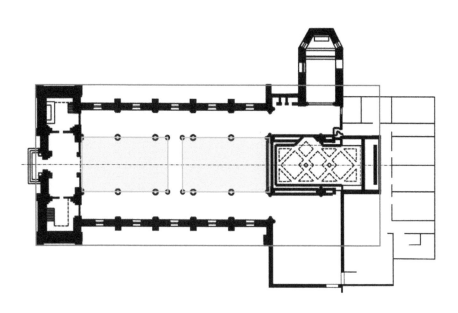

The two Golden Mean Rectangles and the columns

geometry of the transept

The transept was designed using the √5 Rectangle. Inside this rectangle, the Master builder fit three 3x4 Rectangles. Neolithic people employed the famous 3x4 Rectangle in the Carnac region of France for building megalithic structures. One example is the Crucuno quadrilateral that we touched on earlier. It was also employed by Sumerians, Egyptians, Greeks, Romans to build sacred structures.

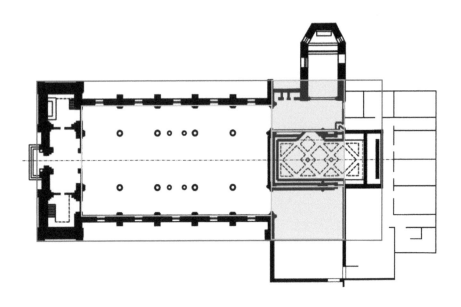

The geometry of the transept with the √5 Rectangle and the 345 Rectangles

Next is a 54/36 Dynamic Rectangle that includes the apse and the transept in its shape. It is the same rectangle as we saw earlier in the nave.

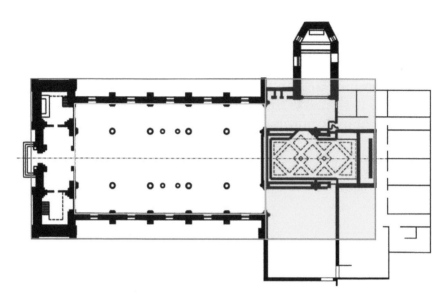

The 54/36 Dynamic Rectangle of the transept

geometry of the apse

Now we will see the masterpiece on the floor of the apse. The apse is the most sacred area of the cathedral, and Master Builder Mouly designed a complex layering of Golden Mean Rectangles which work together to raise the vibration of the apse.

The Dynamic Parthenon Rectangle gives the overall form of the apse. It connects the Solsticial Rectangle of the nave with the √5 Rectangle enveloping the cathedral.

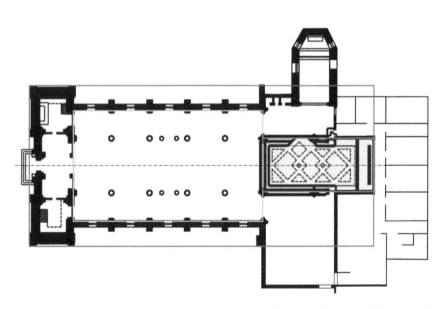

The Parthenon Rectangle and the apse

The beautiful wooden design on the apse floor can be thought of as a geometrical key to the church, left behind by Master Builder Mouly. An apse is a place of high vibration and rarefied energy. Because of this, it is usually a fractal of an important geometrical pattern of the place. As seen in San Miguel, dividing a rectangle or polygon in half, and then in half again creates a figure called the Triple Enclosure. By doing this, the Master Builder enhances the energy and raises the vibration of the place.

The familiar √5 Rectangle enveloping the cathedral was divided by four and used for the shape of the wooden design.

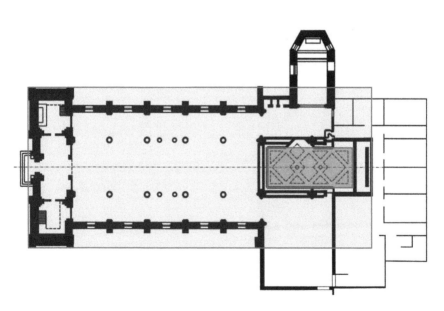

The √5 Rectangle employed in the apse

Several other Dynamic Golden Mean Rectangles were also employed. The Parthenon Rectangle is the violet inner one, the √5 Rectangle is the blue middle one, and outer Double Square Rectangle is red.

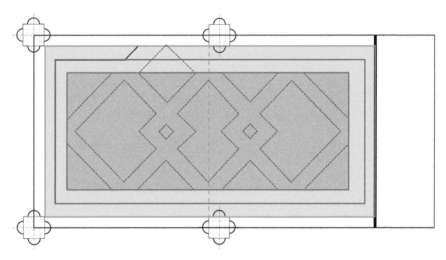

The three main rectangles of the apse, the Double Square Rectangle in red, the √5 Rectangle in blue, and the violet Parthenon Rectangle in the center.

The intricate design in the center is a layering of different sizes of rhombuses found in Santa Fe's solar mandala. Their measurements are no accident, and are another form of using the Triple Enclosure technique to increase spiritual energy.

Mouly's sophisticated use of solar geometry and Golden Mean rectangles in the apse demonstrates his exceptional expertise in the concepts of the Master Builder tradition.

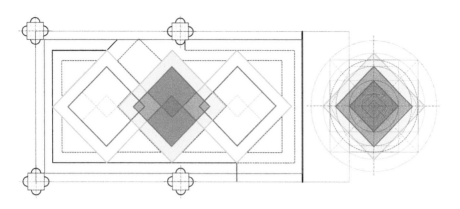

The intricate design of the apse

conclusion

In conclusion, the purpose of the geometry of the Cathedral St. Francis of Assisi was to build an energetical structure connected to the heavens. With the help of Dynamic Rectangles connected to the golden mean, the Cathedral combines divine proportion and the rhythm of the sun. This combination gives the structure more life force energy.

The golden mean is a fractal of the development of life, and the sun's rhythms allow life to grow here on earth. Thus, the Cathedral of St. Francis of Assisi can be seen as a perfect combination of elements dedicated to the sacred, and life.

La Conquistadora, notice she is dressed in light blue
Photo credit: Glenn Nagel, Dreamstime.com

Chapter Five

history of the loretto chapel

Exterior of the Loretto Chapel of Our Lady of Light
Photo credit: Ayla Angelo

Archbishop Jean-Baptiste Lamy brought the architect Master Builder father and son team, Antoine and Projectus Mouly, over from France to build the Cathedral of St Francis. During a lull in building the cathedral due to lack of funds, Lamy suggested the Sisters of Loretto would appreciate the French team's services to build a much-needed chapel for their academy.

Before Antoine returned to France because of blindness in 1874, he had designed the small chapel. His son, Projectus, oversaw the construction until resigning because of criticism and demands to change the chapel's design. To compound this, he unexpectedly passed away in 1878 before completing the chapel, leading to a significant problem. There was no way to access the choir loft above the church floor.

Interior of of the Loretto Chapel
Photo credit: Ayla Angelo

With this, the famous miraculous spiral staircase and its legends began. The Sisters of Loretto called in several carpenters to assist with this problem. The only solution they could come up with was to build a ladder. As this was unacceptable to the Sisters, they began to pray to St Joseph, the patron saint of carpenters. The legend says that on the 9th day of constant praying, a man carrying only a tool box appeared looking for work. He was hired, but wanted to work in secrecy. A few months or in some stories, one day later, the construction was complete. The man disappeared into thin air without ever being paid. Some of the Sisters believed it was St. Joseph himself who had come to aid them in answer to their prayers.

The staircase of Loretto Chapel
Photo credit: Ayla Angelo

In the early 2000s, the mystery was solved by historian Mary J. Straw Cook, who discovered the carpenter was a Frenchman called François-Jean Rochas, who lived in Santa Fe. He had ordered the wood from France. Cook had found an article concerning his death in a newspaper stating he was the craftsman of the staircase. She also discovered records in the Sisters' books revealing a payment made to him for the wood.

The spiral staircase has 33 steps and makes two 360° turns. It was constructed using only wooden pegs, without the use of glue or nails. Part of its mystery is that it was built without a central column or support beams. Originally, it also lacked handrails and was so frightening to descend that some nuns would do so on their hands and knees!

analysis of the subterranean energies

Loretto Chapel follows the classic Master Builder technique of placing the church over a water vein that runs lengthwise down the middle of the church. This water vein is interesting because it is fertility water, a specific type of water frequently used in ancient times. Churches built using these unique waters were usually dedicated to the Virgin.

The two water veins crossing at the entrance are fertility waters, giving an energetic yellow-orange ambiance to the chapel. Fascinatingly enough, the chapel is now mainly used for weddings.

At the crossing of water veins in the center, a lovely blue vortex opens the throat chakra. This beautiful clear blue vortex is the gateway to make the shift into a spiritual connection. Just before arriving at the apse is a little indigo vortex connected to the 3rd eye, which helps prepare for the opening of the crown chakra at the apse.

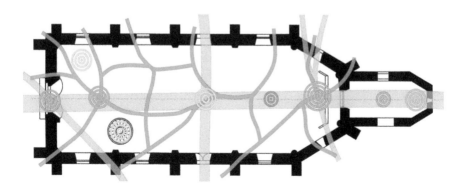

T   he subterranean earth energies of Loretto Chapel
Earth energies drawing by Nicolas Susani

A large violet vortex is located at the apse, resulting from the crossings of the water veins and geological faults. Violet vortexes open the crown chakra and are one of the primary healing energies found in churches. They open the channels of the body and help to make the spiritual connection to the heavens.

The mysterious staircase has an excellent and powerful clear blue vortex due to the geometry utilized in its design.

analysis of the geometry of the place

To begin, having two constructions designed and built by the same Master Builder is rare. Usually, Master Builders construct only one cathedral, which is the masterpiece of their lifetime. It is interesting to see how two separate structures were conceived by Master Builder architect, Antoine Mouly.

For Loretto Chapel, we begin the analysis of the geometry with the apse. It was designed with the familiar hexagonal shape found in many of the Missions of New Mexico. We saw earlier in this book one fine example at the Mission of San Miguel. As discussed before, it is one of the polygons connected to the sun and the Solsticial Rectangle of Santa Fe. The apse is designed using three concentric hexagons, as seen in the illustration below. This shape enhances the powerful violet vortex found there.

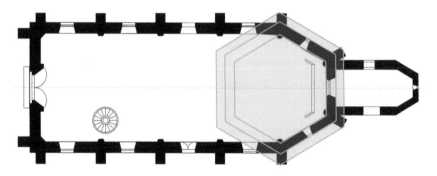

The hexagons employed in the apse of Loretto Chapel

the nave

Looking at the geometry of the nave beginning with the exterior, the entire chapel is enveloped by the Dynamic 1 ÷ 2.752 Rectangle, with its famous Divine Delta Angle.

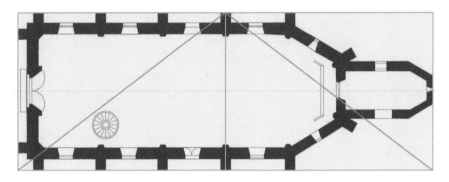

The geometry of the exterior of the chaple and the Divine Delta Angle

Mouly then employed three rectangles to connect with each of the three hexagons of the apse. This connection is a classic technique used by the Master Builders to join the nave to the apse.

The outer hexagon connects to the Solsticial Rectangle of Santa Fe and includes the buttresses. Next, the exterior walls are defined by a Double Square making the connection to the second hexagon. A Double Square is a rectangle that has a √5 diagonal. It is considered one of the oldest rectangles in the western Master Builder tradition, and was employed by the Egyptians, Sumerians, the Hebrews, etc.

The interior walls of the chapel are built using the √5 Rectangle. As we have seen in St. Francis Cathedral, four Solsticial Rectangles of Santa Fe fit inside this remarkable √5 Rectangle. These four Solsticial Rectangles define the position of the columns inside the church.

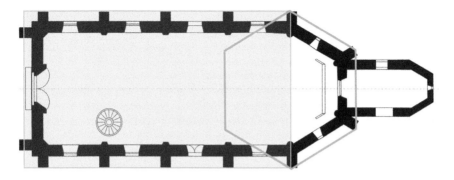

Outer Solsticial Rectangle of Santa Fe and its connection to the hexagon

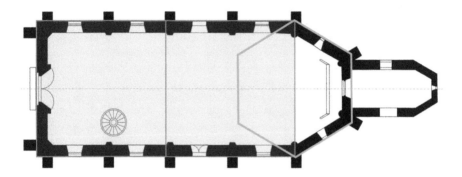

The Double Square Rectangle used for the measurement of the exterior walls and its connection with the hexagon of the apse.

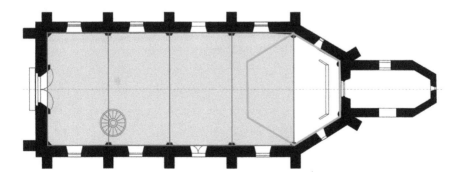

The use of the √5 Rectangle for the interior walls and its connection with the hexagon of the apse

the sacristy

The geometry of the sacristy echoes that of the chapel. It also resembles the Mission of San Miguel and the small chapel of La Conquistadora inside St Francis. It employs two Solsticial Rectangles of Santa Fe, one representing the inside and the other for the outside. These Solsticial Rectangles are combined with hexagons, just as the chapel.

The energy of the apse within the sacristy is a beautiful green heart-opening vortex. It is one of the most potent and beautiful energetic places in the entire chapel. In this place, the chapel earns the name, Our Lady of the Light.

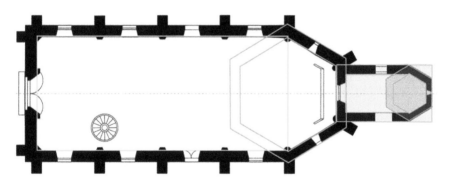

The geometry used in the sacristy

geometry of the exterior elevation

We are fortunate to be able to illustrate how Master Builders worked in three dimensions creating with the Chapel of Loretto. The exterior elevation of Loretto Chapel uses measurements we are familiar with. Mouly primarily worked with the Solsticial Rectangle of Santa Fe, which is also used for the overall exterior height, including the nave and roof.

Exterior of the Loretto Chapel
Photo credit: Ayla Angelo

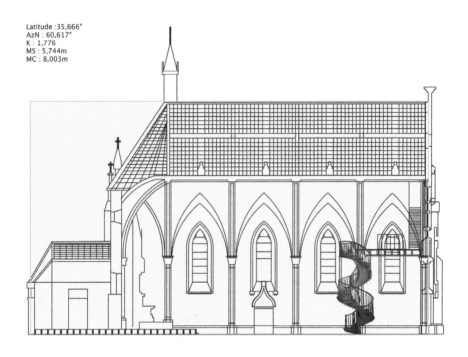

Solsticial Rectangle of Santa Fe and the exterior of the chapel

A Golden Mean Rectangle of 1.618 is used in the apse and sacristy, as can been seen in the illustration on the opposite page.

Finally, the nave and the Solsticial Rectangle can be divided into four √5 Rectangles which fit inside the Solsticial Rectangle of Santa Fe. These √5 Rectangles create the height of the columns and divide the nave into four.

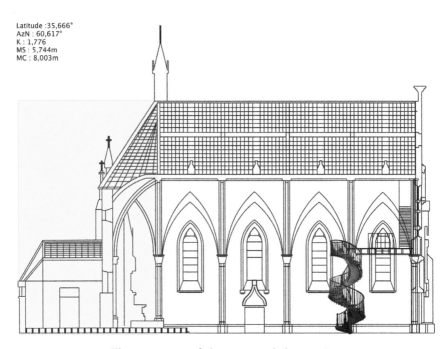

Latitude :35,666°
AzN : 60,617°
K : 1,776
MS : 5,744m
MC : 8,003m

The geometry of the apse and the sacristy

Latitude :35,666°
AzN : 60,617°
K : 1,776
MS : 5,744m
MC : 8,003m

The √5 Rectangles giving the height of the columns

the staircase

The geometry of the staircase is connected to the 7th chakra. The diameter of the staircase and the width of the steps are a measurement associated with the crown chakra. The inner circular upward spiral has the measurement of the element of Fire, which helps to spread spiritual energy throughout the church. The height of the 33 steps which corresponds to the age of Christ, is connected to the element of Ether and the heart chakra.

The staircase of Loretto Chapel
Photo credit: Ayla Angelo

conclusion

Antoine Mouly used the best geometry of Santa Fe for his design of the Loretto chapel. The chapel is intimately connected to the solar mandala of Santa Fe. The use of the hexagon in the apse echoes the work of the Spanish Master Builders of San Miguel and the Chapel of the Conquistadora. Also evident is his expertise and skill in utilizing Dynamic Golden Mean Rectangles to create an ambiance of spirituality, life, and heart-opening energy.

Mouly also took advantage of the classic configuration of earth energies in this chapel, unlike the Cathedral of St. Francis of Assisi. By doing this, his use of geometry magnified the power of the violet apse and green point in the sacristy. We can say that the Chapel of our Lady of Light is truly a masterpiece.

Our Lady of Light inside Loretto Chapel
Photo credit: Ayla Angelo

Conclusion

It is a rare opportunity to study the design and construction by different Master Builder monks and architects in one city. It is fascinating how the European Master Builders adapted their knowledge to serve a different continent. Knowing how to work with the solar rhythms of a new place was evident.

When we began our study in Santa Fe, the Mission of San Miguel was the only church that appeared to have been built by Master Builders. It interested us because it is the oldest church in the United States, and so to our thinking, a Master Builder would have created it. We were right, and as our research deepened, we realized that the European tradition of the Master Builders had continued in Santa Fe throughout the centuries. Even in the 19th century, it was still very much alive, as evidenced by the expertise of Antoine Mouly and his son Projectus.

We hope this book dedicated to the Art of the Master Builders in sacred Santa Fe helps you view holy structures in a different light. In the past, temples and churches were conceived, built, and connected to the sun, the earth, and to life itself. They are indeed living and healing structures. As you have seen in these pages, many hidden geometrical treasures are concealed in their construction. The Mission of San Miguel, the Shrine of Our Lady of Guadalupe, the Cathedral of St. Francis of Assisi, and the Loretto Chapel are four excellent examples found in the United States. The city of Santa Fe can be proud of having such beautiful examples of the art of building sacred structures.

The Mission of San Miguel
Photo credit: Giban59, Dreamstime.com

Appendix

solsticial rectangles

A Solsticial Rectangle is connected to the sun's rhythms throughout the year by the winter and summer solstice sunrises and sunsets.

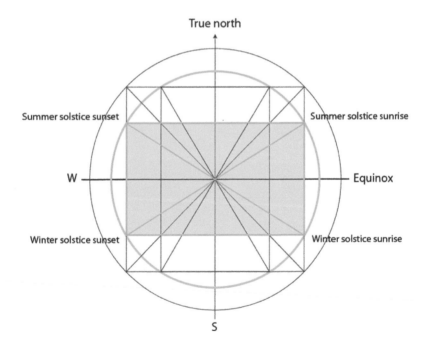

The Solsticial Rectangle

santa fe's solsticial rectangle

Santa Fe's Solsticial Rectangle is extraordinary because of its relationship with the golden √5 Rectangle. It was rare for the European Master Builders to work with a latitude having a double connection with this Dynamic Rectangle. That is, four Santa Fe Solsticial Rectangles fit inside the √5 Rectangle and four √5 Rectangles fit inside the Santa Fe Solsticial Rectangle!

The √5 Rectangle can be thought of as the quintessence of the Golden Mean and its connection to life. Combining it with the Solsticial Rectangle of Santa Fe creates a rare and sacred relationship with the sun. Perhaps this is one of the reasons we can say that Santa Fe is indeed sacred.

√5 Rectangle with four Santa Fe Solsticial Rectangles inside

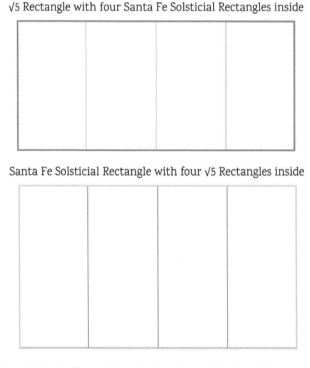

Santa Fe Solsticial Rectangle with four √5 Rectangles inside

Sacred Santa Fe and its relationship with the √5 Rectangle

solsticial rectangles often used building churches

The Master Builders used three main Solsticial Rectangles with reference to Christianity for church design until around the 19th century. The Jerusalem Solsticial Rectangle is the primary example, being the birthplace of Christ. Its proportions evolved over time because the angle of the earth's ecliptic (the plane of the earth's orbit around the sun) changes. For example, in the 3rd century, the ratio was 1.87. In the 11th century, it was 1.876, and in the 17th century, it was 1.885.

Mother Mary was significant as well, as she spent her last days in Ephesus. The Master Builders employed this Solsticial Rectangle to connect a church to the energy of the Virgin. For example, most churches dedicated to Mary use this Solsticial Rectangle in their construction. The nave uses the Ephesus Rectangle in the Shrine of Our Lady of Guadalupe. The ratio for Ephesus is 1.70 to 1.71.

Using the Solsticial Rectangle of Rome, the Master Builders connected the church to the Vatican and the Pope. Sometimes Rome's Solsticial Rectangle is confused with the Golden Mean Rectangle because their proportions are very close. The ratio for Rome in the 18th century was 1.58, and the Golden Mean Rectangle was 1.618.

Solsticial Rectangle of Jerusalem

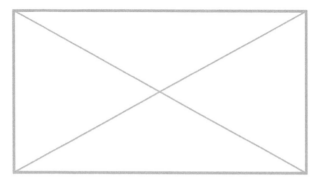

Solsticial Rectangle of Ephesus

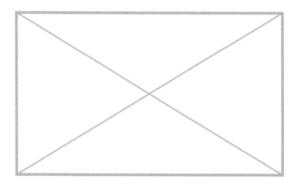

Solsticial Rectangle of Rome

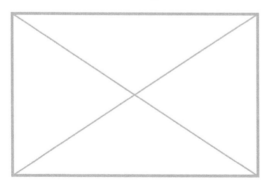

Three main Solsticial Rectangles employed in churches

dynamic rectangles

A Dynamic Rectangle is a rectangle that has a relationship with the golden ratio. The most recognizable Golden Mean Rectangle has a proportion of 1.618. The golden mean and its fantastic sequence of numbers of 1.618 and 5/3, 8/5, 13/8, 21/13...was known and employed by the Egyptians. The first written definition dates back to the Greek mathematician Euclid (325-256BC). The popularity of this ratio took off during the Renaissance in the 15th century after the publication of the book of Luca Pacioli, *The Divine Proportion,* and was used as a guideline for the aesthetics of beauty in art and geometry.

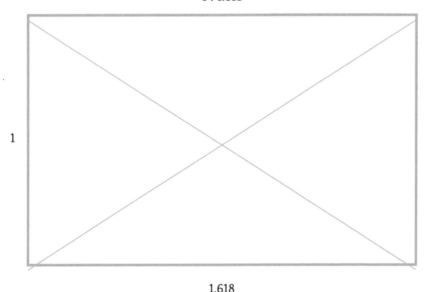

The Golden Ratio 1 : 1.618

The first Dynamic Rectangle is called the Cheops Rectangle and has a ratio of 1:1.272. It was employed to build the Cheops Pyramid by using two right-angle triangles shown in the illustration below. In the Sanctuario de Nuestra Señora de Guadalupe in Santa Fe, the Cheops Rectangles are represented in the sides of the transept.

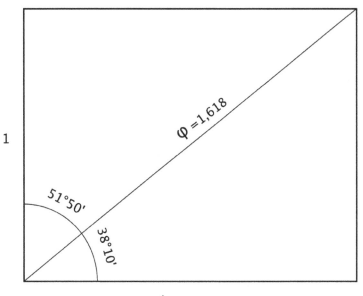

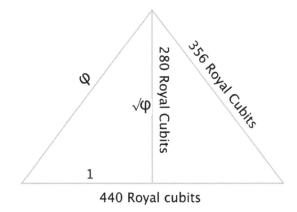

The Cheops Dynamic Rectangle 1 : 1.272

The second Dynamic Rectangle is 1:1.376, also called the 54/36. This rectangle was used in paintings during the Renaissance by Italian, French, and Dutch painters. The angles of this rectangle are 36° and 54°. The hypotenuse and the long side of the resulting right triangles are in the ratios 2/Φ and Φ/2. That is to say 1.236 and 0.809 respectively.

1 : 1.376 or 54/36

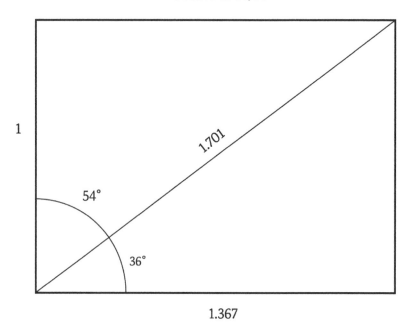

The 1 : 1.376 Dynamic Rectangle

The third Dynamic Rectangle is 1:1.538 or 72°. This rectangle is related to the decagon and pentagon by its angles and proportions. Because the decagon is linked to the DNA and life, this rectangle is too.

The two half-diagonals, EB and EC, form an angle of 36° (18 + 18). Their length divided by the dimension equals Φ. EB / BC = Φ, shown in the illustration on the next page.

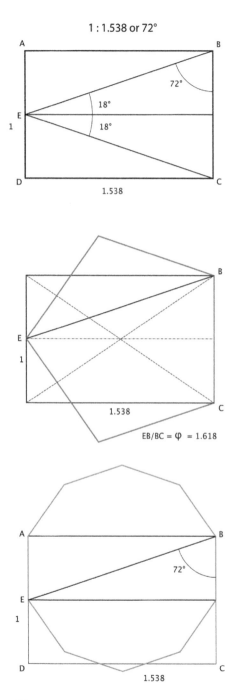

1 : 1.538 or 72°

1.538

EB/BC = φ = 1.618

The 1 : 1.538 or 72° Dynamic Rectangle

The fourth Dynamic Rectangle is the Golden Mean Rectangle, Phi Φ. The dimensions of this rectangle are the proportion 1.618, called Divine Proportion or Rectangle Phi, and employed for sacred constructions. Used in Egyptian structures such as the Tomb of Petosiris from 300BC, it can also be seen in the Parthenon, 400BC, and the Pyramid of Quetzalcoatl at Tula, Mexico, 800AD.

In terms of energy, the Golden Mean Rectangle must never be employed by itself, because it disconnects one from the essential connection to the earth. It is best utilized with Solar Geometry as the Greeks did in the Parthenon. In churches, it is often confused with the Solsticial Rectangle of Rome 1.585, which is close to the ratio of 1.618.

1 : 1.618

1.618

Divine Ratio or Rectangle Phi 1 : 1.1618

The fifth rectangle is called the Double Square or the 2:1 Rectangle. It consists of two squares side by side. Found engraved in Sumerians tablets dating back to around 3000BC, it is a very old rectangle. Mentioned in the Bible as the Silver Rectangle, it was used in sacred construction as one of the pillars of ancient geometry. The Double Square is linked to quadrature and the Fire element. To see the golden ratio in the 2:1 Rectangle, add the diagonal of √5 (2.236) to 1, divide by two, and you get 1.618. Using the diagonal makes it possible to find the famous √5 Rectangle.

2 : 1

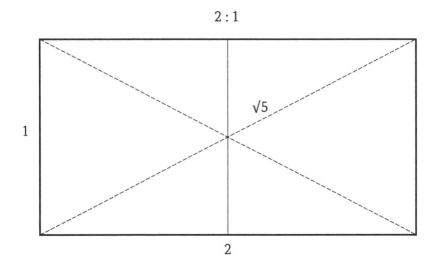

The Double Square of 2 : 1

The sixth Dynamic Rectangle is the Parthenon Rectangle, with a ratio of 1:2.164. This rectangle is characterized by the ratio of the diagonals and the half diagonal BD/BE = Φ.

Standing atop the Athens Acropolis, the Parthenon Rectangle is the stylobate, which is the stepped platform upon which the columns are placed in the temple of Athena Parthenos, the Virgin.

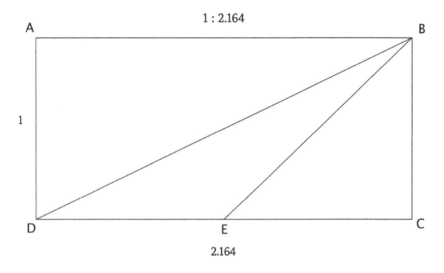

The Dynamic Rectangle of 1 : 2.164 or the Parthenon Rectangle

The seventh Dynamic Rectangle is the famous √5 Rectangle, found by using the diagonal of the Double Square. It was well-known to the Babylonians, Assyrians, Egyptians, and Greeks. Framing the central square are two Φ Rectangles. When the Rectangle Φ (AGDH) is joined to the square, it forms another Rectangle Φ (ABCD). The √5 Rectangle can be found on facades of Greek temples and on the pedestal of the Parthenon.

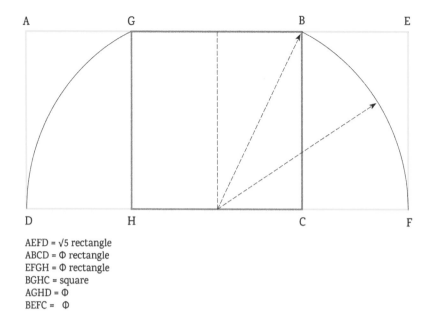

AEFD = √5 rectangle
ABCD = Φ rectangle
EFGH = Φ rectangle
BGHC = square
AGHD = Φ
BEFC = Φ

The Dynamic √5 Rectangle

The eighth Dynamic Rectangle has the Divine Delta angle and the ratio of 1:2.752. It consists of two rectangles 2√Φ, which have angles of 54°and 36°. DC/DE = Φ

This rectangle is especially remarkable for highlighting the Divine Triangle and its sublime angle of 108°. An excellent example of this is found at the Basilica of Vezélay, dedicated to Mary Magdalene, in France. Over the door, Christ is depicted with his arms outstretched with his hands and head forming the Divine Delta angle. It can also be found on the façade of the Cathedral of Auch in France.

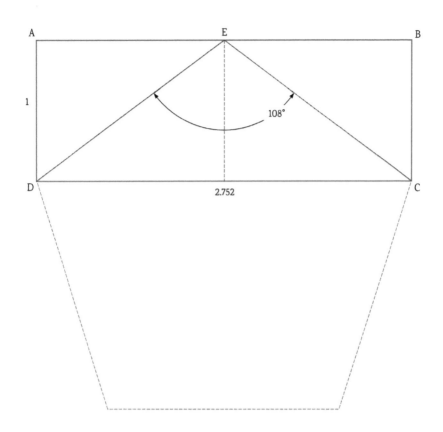

The angle of the Divine Delta and 1 : 2.752 rectangle

static rectangles

The Square is a polygon with four equal sides and four right angles. In the tradition of the European Master Builders, it is the foundation of geometry. It represents earth and matter.

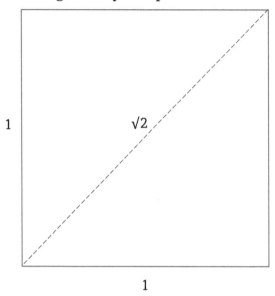

The Square

The 3:4 Rectangle comes from the scalene triangle of 3:4:5, as we can see on the illustration on the next page. The 3:4:5 Triangle is also called the Isiac Triangle in honor of the Goddess Isis.

Since the dawn of time, the 3:4:5 Triangle has been one of the first Right Triangles used by builders because of its simple ratios of 3, 4, and 5 to construct right angles of great precision.

The Cromlech of Crucuno, and the table stone of the Dolmen Mane er R'hoech, have the proportions of the 3:4:5 Rectangle. In the 1960s, the Kergall Research Group in France, demonstrated that the Right Triangle of 3:4:5 was used to position the megaliths in Brittany.

It was so popular in the Middle Ages that Master Builders used a rope for measuring the 3:4:5 Rectangle called the Druidic cord or 12-knot rope. Because of the superstition of 13, the rope became known as the 12-knot rope alluding to the 12 spaces instead of 13 knots. Worn as a belt, it served as an instrument for tracing and measuring the one cubit space between the knots.

Master Builders also employed a "cane" with notches or marks which allowed measurements such as the palm, span, foot, and cubit. With the use of the 12-knot rope and the cane, the Master Builder was provided with the necessary tools to trace the designs on the ground to build a church or cathedral. The Franciscan monks used these two tools for building the first churches in Santa Fe.

3:4:5 Rectangle

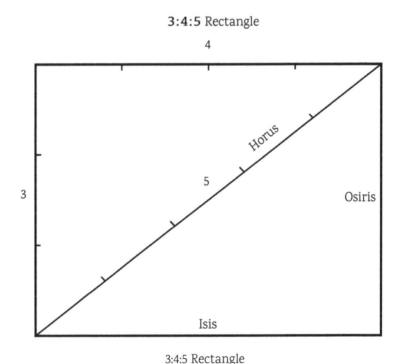

3:4:5 Rectangle

1:3 Solomon Rectangle as illustrated below, is a Triple Square and was thought to be the structure of Solomon's temple. The diagonal is √10, and its value of 3.16 is very close to Pi.

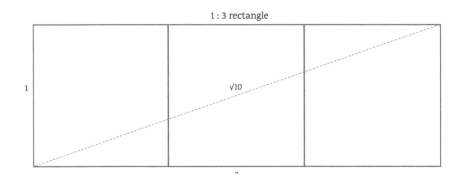

Solomon's Rectangle or 1 : 3

Bibliography

Ad Quadratum by Fredrik Macody Lund, William Brown & Co, Limited London 1921

The Cathedral Basilica of St. Francis of Assisi our Parish History PDF, www.ebsfa.org/parish-life/about/ accessed 6/2/21

De Re Aedificatoria by Leon Battista Alberti, Gallica BNF Florence 1485

Eglise Romane, Chemin de Lumiere by R. Montercy and J. Bonvin, Mosaique 1983

The Guadalupe Church – Santa Fe, New Mexico by Joshua Trujillo, https://www.myguadalupe.com/guadalupe-church.html Accessed 9/10/21

La Divine Proportion by Luca Pacioli, Compagnonage 1980

Leonard da Vinci, Oeuvre Peinte et Graphique by Frank Zollner, Taschen 2007

The Legend Behind the 'Miraculous Staircase' by Marie Kester, https://historyofyesterday.com/the-legend-behind-the-miraculous-staircase-70b8b1e58c91 accessed 9/3/21

Les Cahiers du Nombre d'or V. Le Parthenon by Elisa Maillard, Tournon et Cie 1968

Loretto Chapel SAH Archipedia, www.sah-archipedia.org/ buildings/NM-01-049-0174, accessed 9/3/21

Secrets of Sacred Geometry; Solar Geometry for Health and Life by Anne Z. Parker, Karen Crowley-Susani, and Dominique Susani, Triple Enclosure Publishing 2018

The Medieval Sketchbook of Villard de Honnecourt by Villard de Honnecourt Dover Fine Art, History of Art English Edition

The Missions of New Mexico Since 1776; Santa Fe: La Parroquia PDF, www.npshistory.com/publications/kessell/nm-missions/ arroquia.htm, accessed 8/9/21

Sanctuaries of Spanish New Mexico by Marc Treib, University of California Press Berkeley and Los Angeles 1993

Tlaxcalan Indians in New Mexico PDF by Stanley A. Lucero M.A.T., www.lucerito.net Revised 2009

Vitruve, De l'architecture texte en latin et traduit en français par Ch. L. Maufras, Gallica BNF 1847

Les Yantras by Louis Rosier, publication personnelle 1992

CPSIA information can be obtained
at www.ICGtesting.com
Printed in the USA
LVHW070223180422
716448LV00004B/7